How to gain Power and Authority?

By

Chakrapani Srinivasa

How to gain Power and Authority?

By

Chakrapani Srinivasa

Dedicated to My Dear Parents

About the Author

Chakrapani Srinivasa (Padmaja), Freelance journalist from India possesses Bachelor degree in Engineering (B.E) and Post graduate in Business Management (MBA) with Distinction. He has worked as Associate Editor of 'Naradar' fortnightly journal in Chennai, India. He is the Senior Editor of the journal "The Divineness".

Contributed articles, short stories and travelogues in leading journals like Ananda Vikatan, Kumudam, Savi, Kalki, Dinamani Kadhir, Dinamani daily, Idhayam Pesukirathu, Naradar etc

He has written articles and e books through Smashwords Inc, Kindle Direct Publishing, Atlanta publications, Cooperjal publications (UK), lulu.com, ezinearticles.com, shvoong.com, iproclaim.com (USA) and TCC news (Germany).

He is the Consulting Editor: Contemporary Who's Who-Research Board of Advisors of ABI.

View his other books
https://www.amazon.com/-/e/B01G3JTQ92

Preface

Great companies have fallen hopelessly behind the change curve because middle managers and first level employees lacked the power and courage to speak up.

To be an activist and to exercise power enormous courage and willpower are needed for persons at bottom level to raise his voice, breaking the hierarchy.

The goal is not to leave senior executive behind.

The goal is not to stage a palace coup.

But when senior managers are distracted, when planning has supplanted strategizing, and when more energy is being devoted to protecting the past than to creating the future, activists come forward and enforce power.

Contents

Courage and Strength

"Great leaders operate through power of his total self and his holistic vision of life".

Self Knowledge, self acceptance and self esteem together have powerful impact on the person.

They provide him with

- The courage to surround himself with the best people – People who are leaders in their own right.

- The strength to face reality however discouraging

- Resilience and openness to accept to honest feedback

- Do what is required for the benefit of the organization.

With the power inborn in them or built out of sheer experience power plays a vital tool in any administration.

This power provides a good

- Vision
- Strategy
- Commitment
- Involvement
- Charisma
- Fame
- Self confidence
- Fruitful spirit

Power gives a fear to the subordinates.

It makes them dumbfounded, speechless and invalid.

Nikita Khrushchev, after he become president of the Supreme Society, gave a speech to a large group of Communist Party leaders in which he denounced the excesses of Stalin.

During a pause, a voice rang out from the back of the hall "You were there. Why didn't you stop him?"

Taken aback by such impertinence Khrushchev thundered "Who said that?"

There was tremendous Power in his voice.

The questioner sunk low in his seat and was silent.

After a long and uncomfortable minute in which his eyes raked the audience, Khrushchev replied

"Now You Know Why?"

It is often safer to be silent.

So, power makes other dead.

A deadly silence prevails when power predominates.

All barriers are shattered.

Nothing can stand against its odds.

Power is powerful weapon.

To be an activist one must care more for one's community than for one's position in the hierarchy.

Great companies have fallen hopelessly behind the change curve because middle managers and first level employees lacked the power and courage to speak up.

To be an activist and to exercise power enormous courage and willpower are needed for persons at bottom level to raise his voice, breaking the hierarchy.

The goal is not to leave senior executive behind.

The goal is not to stage a palace coup.

But when senior managers are distracted, when planning has supplanted strategizing, and when more energy is being devoted to protecting the past than to creating the future, activists come forward and enforce power.

So, power not only comes from top but also from bottom line at time of crisis.

It is not a personal revolution against a leader but a bold step to avoid calamity.

Nelson was involved in a battle and his commander ordered that if he gives a signal with his red flag, shooting must be stopped and immediately get retreated.

Battle was proceeding.

Opponent was forceful and many of Nelson's ships sunk.

Seeing the calamity his commander showed waved a red flag to stop the battle.

Nelson's subordinates immediately alerted Nelson!

But Nelson took out his telescope and with his blind eye, which he lost in one of several battles; he viewed and said "I cannot see any signal. Shoot the enemy. Continue!"

With tremendous power he waged and won that battle.

He was honored and made the chief.

Power springing out of will power and confidence will fetch fruits.

The hierarchy even in battle field, when broken by Nelson fetched a glorious success.

Power in him brought and showered laurels to achieve goals.

In any organization the Power helps to successfully break with the past – in strategy, structure processes and products and adapt to the demands made by the eco-logical niches, which they occupy.

As environment changes so must the businesses.

Only business hours, which can acquire momentum of change, will be able to sustain it in future.

A good power at the top will give new strategies, planning techniques and templates of new initiatives in entering new markets and growing new products.

If power is negligible then the chaotic condition will spring and put the firm to disaster.

Power is an intangible and elusive process in an organization but its effect can be felt.

The following consequences occur with power in an organization:

-Gaining a lead in budget outlay compared to other departments.

By executing power, a Regional Manager in a leading company was able to get a fund of Rs. 2 crores for remodeling and refurnishing their Chennai regional office, whereas such amount was not allocated for branches in Nagpur or Allahabad.

The Regional Manager was a powerful candidate in the management's view point.

-Achievement in production schedules:

In another MNC, a branch in Hyderabad unit reached a maximum production in leather and sales of consumer items.

That was mainly due to power with a background support of some local politicians.

-Certain demands can be put into management's agenda to fulfill the needs.

In another leading company, several North Indian staffs were recruited and as their number increased an agenda was placed in the board meeting stating that the canteen facilities should be increased and special cook on Tandoori items, North Indian dish specialists are to be added.

As the North Indian Candidates and staff were powerful, the agenda was moved favorably to them.

The canteen facilities were enhanced to cater their needs.

The number of individuals making a demand also enforces power.

In recruitment too power politics come into the foreground.

A talented staff and vital department head in the software testing divisions in a multi-crore group in Bangalore was able to get recruitment for his friends.

He was holding a powerful post and key areas were under his control.

Also in a public sector, Chairman's close associate was posted as Special officer on Duty to head and have a vigil on several issues.

This indicates power.

They said it was management's discretion.

Even in a leading University and other private owned Universities, the Dean, HOD, board members have seat allocations in professional courses.

These are indicators of power.

-Acquiring additional men, materials and amenities going out of the way are all indicators of power.

-Out of turn in promotions can also be obtained by power. A background in political or in the management can give an uplift with the result of power.

Authority

Hierarchy

Authority is related to power but narrower in scope.

It is focused by the formal hierarchy and reporting relationships and power is associated with one's post or position in the organization.

The formal authority is exercised only in downward direction – from top to bottom; from General Manager to Deputy General Manager.

The properties that pinpoints authority:

-The post held and the personal charisma springs out authority.

-If a Chief Engineer commands, it is immediately obeyed by the Deputy Chief Engineer because he is in the rank below him.

Water flows from higher level to lower level.

So also authority!

His senses command him to obey since the order issued is an 'authorized one'.

Chief Engineer has got every right to command and give instruction and it is the duty of his immediate subordinate along with others has to obey.

Formation of hierarchy top to bottom exists and authority exists along the formal chain of command.

In a popular MNC the scenario is different.

When an Rs500 crores collaboration with an Italian firm had to be signed, the Managing Director waited for the instruction and green signal from the Chairman.

But the Chairman coolly said "My instructions are not needed. Do what I will do if I were you".

He did it.

The collaboration was a big success for that company.

Authority bypassed was proficient and work out well.

"Trust gives trust" says an economist.

Therefore Hierarchy failed but net result was success – a glorious success.

In the present business school trends, graduates, brimming with pride and talents come out of it and when they enter the business houses, they don't bother about the authority formalities.

They don't expect the boss to exercise his authority to command him.

In one of the south Indian auto manufacturing group Board Meeting, M.D questioned

"What is your contribution to this company"?

The MBA from IIM immediately quipped.

"What are your contributions?"

Such is the trend now.

Bold and brave soldier like youngster don't halt or patiently wait for hierarchical authority to overshadow them.

They shoot up at all occasions and they prove that they are:

- Right
- Might and
- Perfectionist

Their skill and IIM school knowledge makes them sit straight and express counterviews against the management.

Authority also arises during emergency conditions.

In a public sector company when operators were under strike, certain executives were authorized to drive the vehicles for running the organization.

So, they obtained authority out of crisis.

In another concern, where army equipments and telecommunication gadgets are manufactured, only few are authorized to enter the documentation center where several data are stored.

So, authority arises due to national safety.

In large organizations for materials purchase and procurement of spare parts only certain people are authorized to sign.

The authority arises due to reliability and post.

Another point to be noted is authority cannot be exercised easily on some people if they have a political support or union support.

If authority is forced then a lay off or tool down strike may fire out causing disruption in the normal proceedings.

Hence even though by hierarchy a person exerts authority, certain barriers hinder them from doing it.

Power cannot be exercised by holding a post in an organization.

-Personal charisma

-Additional knowledge

-Immaculate style

-Access to vital information

-Decide one's power in a given situation.

"Power to influence through uplifting the consciousness of people get them to commit to the purpose and thereby make them transfer their energies in that direction, has been one of the remarkable characteristics of transformational leaders"

Organizational Control and Major Control Strategies

The crucial indicator to the likelihood of a business group's survival in the face of competition is the evidence of the emergence of strategy and control.

The generic choice for today's business group is between cost-leadership and product focus as it strives to attain the distinctive, inimitable competitive edge.

That is the hallmark of corporations that can keep rivals at arm's length.

The proof that such a choice is being made for every business, improves the prospects of a group.

Conversely, the absence of such decisions implies that the business in question have no defined distinctiveness, and offer little by way of unmatched value to the customer.

Vital too is the assertion of strategic intent in a group's plans. Is it for instance going global or at least, pursuing global scale?

Strategic Quotient

Has it made innovation and customer focus the bedrock of all its activities?

Is it weaving speed, flexibility and quick response time into the very fabric of all its actions?
The features that a business house with a clear strategy in place demonstrates are the obvious measures for the group's strategic quotient.

Thus its cost position vis-à-vis rivals, supported by backward linkages to operations reveal whether not it is aiming to provide the lowest prices in the market place.

Strategic Positioning

Alternatively, the businesses that make uniqueness its strategic plan must invest and deliver differentiated products that competitor cannot match.

And most important, the determination to persist with its strategic positioning is visible in its efforts to build competitive advantages at every stage of the value chain.

Good control leads to serving the multiple purposes of generating cash flow for new investments, of targeting emerging high-growth opportunities of keeping pace with changing trends in consumer demand and of allowing the group to leverage its core strength.

The higher the contribution to the total turnover made by stable business, ideally with high market shares in low growth, low competition markets the more solid is the foundation of group for survival in future.

An efficient control on organization should create a balance between businesses that will generate funds and those that will demand investments with a skew on either side weakening the survival potential.

Operational Efficiency

The quest for operational efficiency aimed at squeezing every drop of redundancy out of the organization is a bid not only to contain costs, but also to optimize product quality is an ongoing one around the world.

Management Control

When it comes to gauging the effectiveness of a business house at improving its operation, it is both the effort and the results that count.

First, the use and frequency of techniques like bench marking, total quality management, just-in-time inventory management, business process re-engineering, supply chain management or customer and employee surveys are essential indicators of attempt to sharpen operation.

A good strategy in control fetches fruits in operational efficiency.

That is an indicator of sound management and good control.

Finances

It is the life and blood of the business house for survival, essential for circulating strategies and capabilities, the ability to bankroll posterity.

 The financial depth of a business group is really a measure of its competence for making new investments when necessary for ensuring healthy each flow year after year, for having the capacity to withstand hard times without having to put its assets into stock.

The real muscle that proves financial strength, therefore, is the potential of the business house for raising and servicing capital.

A good control in organization and sound strategy creates a healthy 'muscle'.

"Those in a position of power should be in a position to control and grow".

War Gaming

To meet the competition and good organization control, action learning is vital.

Malcolm Baldrige Quality Awards Bradley Gate recommends, "Create a war room in your corporate headquarters – displaying on the walls information about market perceived price profiles, competitor information and analytical charts – to help what is called Action learning".

A Management theoretician says "Confidence is what is right with an ignorance of what really works".

That scathing indictment forms the basis of the present thinking on war gaming which hold that only the reality of the market place can provide the details that "Strategy must be built on".

The basis for such thinking:

First forecasting assumes that the part will repeat itself and is, thus no longer applicable as the rate of change in the environment increases.

Second strategic planners; mistakenly assume that the world will wait while they plan in a detailed manner.

Finally strategists believe that they can program and simulate the innovation process, which is debatable.

Scenario planning, which is the other alternative suffers from the limitation that it usually fails to capture, the scenario that actually evolves.

The option therefore, is to play war games.

By control and vital strategies managers will learn to make better decisions, identity critical gaps in their information bank, anticipate competitors moves, suggest ways to pre-empt or react to them limit surprises and identify your weaknesses and strengths.

The War Game

Identify the conditions and situations to be simulated.

-Form teams to represent your competitors

- Begin the game by initiating moves and counter moves

- Conduct interim analyzer to improve understanding of the dynamics

- Make an inventory of out comes under different scenarios

- Translate findings into alternative action plans for the future

Creating Systems

Every corporation is assailed at intervals by unexpected crises that could blow them out of existence.

Don't expect to forestall such events!

Mostly occurring in the external environment, they build up momentum with either the ferocity of a twister or the feline grace of a tiger.

The best that companies can do is to setup system and create a culture that considers it extremely likely that such a blow will smile them at any time.

This control through systems always works.

"A Good CEO'S strength lies in controlling through systems while he plays the overall strategy!"

Men may come and men may go, but systems remain to control the organizations.

It should be so designed that anyone who comes in and go out is guided to smoothen the operations in an organization.

Control through Good Leadership

What are the qualities that will distinguish the leadership of a business house that survives from that of one which goes under?

Speed and efficiency of response, the articulations of an over-reaching but cogent vision and the charisma to rise above the role of the feudal head are crucial components.

So is the propensity for championing change, being forthright and decisive, and the ability to resolve conflicts.

And most of all it is the aptitude for conducting a group of diverse managers into an orchestra playing a single melody that makes for quality leadership.

A good strategy should lay a good foundation for control and efficient leadership.

Cost Strategy

Corner stone of an organization's strategy lies in sharpening its cost efficiencies to maintain its position as the lowest cost producer.

It should leverage low prices-high quality. A focus on keeping cost under control and boosting productivity is important.

Economies of Scale

A largest producer of three wheelers in the world says,

"I knew that, one day we would have competition and that we would have to be ready for it. Before that happens I wanted build volumes".

The benefits of being big are that it allows a company to buy cheap from a well developed vendor-base as well as benefit from a large dealer network – which are crucial.

"The company gets very big old and fuddy-duddy. It also becomes bureaucratic and conservative, preferring the status quo.

These are the huge and real diseconomies of scale".

Visions

"Where there is no vision people perish".

-The Bible.

An organizational vision offers a compelling method and control for forging employees into an empowered, highly motivated team.

It adds purpose to employee's lives, outlives changes of guard, and is the corner –stone of the strategic architecture of a truly successful organization.

The organization must be rational and creative, cerebral and passionate, demanding yet friendly.

That's where Vision comes in!

Working and controlling without vision is like putting together a jigsaw puzzle without having the picture before you.

Moses used the vision of a land of milk and honey to motivate his people to set off for the Promised Land.

Vision is an inspirational picture of a future that can be created, offering clarity amidst confusion, hope amidst despair and unit of purpose amongst diversity of personal causes.

Other books by the same author

Strange India
https://www.amazon.co.uk/dp/B07S73LCTK

Kohlinoor of India: Winner Virat Kohli
https://www.amazon.co.uk/dp/B07SKNRVCT

Never Forgotten Naradar Srinivasa Rao: Most Enterprising Journalist
https://www.amazon.co.uk/dp/B07NLFY73C

How to Manage Funds in an Organization?
https://www.amazon.co.uk/dp/B00Z0Q8IF8

Wonders of Nano Technology
https://www.amazon.co.uk/dp/B07D3ZP7MC

https://www.amazon.com/dp/B08BF4HCVX

What are the Best HRD Tactics?

https://www.amazon.co.uk/dp/B07HZ7JK18

Solar Energy Plans in Tamilnadu

https://www.amazon.co.uk/dp/B01G44ZL4K

How to Forecast Manpower Needs in an Organization: You Have The Skill!

https://www.amazon.co.uk/dp/B0111GBZKK

Infrastructure in India

https://www.amazon.co.uk/dp/B0163777RW

Accountant's Role in an Organization: A book for Accountants

https://www.amazon.co.uk/dp/B00YYHDHU0

Inland Waterways and Hydro Power in India

https://www.amazon.co.uk/dp/B015NEZMXW

Quiz and General Knowledge

https://www.amazon.co.uk/dp/B01N4M99S7

In Search of Paradise and Peace

https://www.amazon.co.uk/dp/B07C7F3XKM

Graphene -The God of Nano Technology

https://www.amazon.co.uk/dp/B07561LWTT

HRD Systems and Management by Objectives

https://www.amazon.co.uk/dp/B016UC9UKC

International Conferences on Nanotechnology in India

https://www.amazon.co.uk/dp/B07BP8YLJZ

Holy Madhwa Saints: Get Divine Pleasure by Reading

https://www.amazon.co.uk/dp/B010WNBYU4

Trade Shows in India and Participants

https://www.amazon.co.uk/dp/B016PV1KS8

How to Plan Career and Quality Discipline in an Organization? Plan for Prosperity

https://www.amazon.co.uk/dp/B011GXOXIE

How to Speak Skillfully?
https://www.amazon.com/dp/B08BJ8PCKT

How to Supervise Efficiently?
https://www.amazon.com/dp/B08BNFYSPQ- e book
https://www.amazon.com/dp/B08BR8YYG6?ref_=pe_3052080_397514860

How to Develop Systems for Profit?

https://www.amazon.com/dp/B08BYVL2P9

Nanotechnology Research in India

https://www.amazon.com/dp/B08BZDFVR8

How to Create a Turnaround in Your Organization?

https://www.amazon.com/dp/B08C97X2F9?ref_=pe_3052080_397514860

What are the Best Strategies for your Company to Grow?

https://www.amazon.com/dp/B08CC8Z9F9

How to Plan and Control Successfully?

https://www.amazon.com/dp/B08CRSTW38

How to become a Talented Manager?

https://www.amazon.com/dp/B08DNWKLL2

How to Win the Grace of God?

https://www.amazon.com/dp/B08DL1LMTZ

Tutorial and Hand book for Accountants

https://www.amazon.com/dp/B08DVCHNX9

Jokes & Satire

https://www.amazon.com/dp/B08DYB73Z3

How to become a Leader?

https://www.amazon.com/gp/product/B08BF4HCVX

How to Handle Conflicts and Collective Bargaining?

https://www.amazon.com/dp/B08F2JKB5J

How to Tackle Collaboration and Intervention?

https://www.amazon.com/dp/B08F23HDRT

Click to see my e books published by Amazon

https://www.amazon.com/-/e/B01G3JTQ92